You Only Live Once

LIVE FOR GOD

Mary Olufunmilayo Adekson

NEW HARBOR PRESS

RAPID CITY, SD

Adekson/New Harbor Press
1601 Mt. Rushmore Rd. Ste 3288
Rapid City, SD 57701
www.NewHarborPress.com

Ordering Information:
Quantity sales. Special discounts are available on quantity purchases by corporations, associations, and others. For details, contact the "Special Sales Department" at the address above.

You Only Live Once: Live for God / Mary Olufunmilayo Adekson. -- 1st ed.
ISBN 978-1-63357-319-2

This book is first dedicated: To God Almighty: The Creator, Giver and Preserver of life who gave me the inspiration, opportunity and long life to write and finish this book. To You be all the glory. Excellent God !

To my earthly father, late Papa Gabriel Omodele Ekundiya Asanbe-Williams, of excellent memory, whose unconditional love for me, solidified my thirsty love for my Heavenly Father. "The righteous shall be in everlasting remembrance" (Psalm 112:6b)

To all those who call God Almighty their Father and who calls Jesus Christ their Savior

To all those who will accept the Lord Jesus Christ as their Savior after reading "You only live once: Live for God !"

Contents

Preface

There is nobody like Our Heavenly Father. He is All-Knowing, He is Omnipresent, Omnipotent and Omniscient (Psalm 139:7-12, 13-18 & 1-6). God is undeniably Great ! He is the Living God whose power can never be surpassed. His power is undeniable and nobody and nothing can stand in His way when He wants to bless His children. I am a living witness that God's power is insurmountable and cannot be suppressed. We will leave that story for another day. Who is like unto Thee O God ! Who is like unto thee ! O God! Among the gods who is like thee ! Glorious in holiness and fearful in praises ! Doing wonders : Halleluia ! (Exodus 15:11).

Thank you for picking up this book. My intended audience are everyone who wants to live fully for God and those who thirsts for God's grace in their hearts. The young, the middle aged and the old will like this book because it will speak to those things that are important in life. Afterall we only live once. Living for God is not all that complicated. It just needs putting our hearts into it. This book is therefore out to inspire, teach and encourage you its readers.

"You only live once live for God" will encourage, chastise and admonish individuals of all ages and works of life who are thirsty for God's inspiration and direction. This book will share God's promises that will ebb God's joy in you as you peruse the pages and also point you to the glory set before you here and in the life after. The book will be your companion as you navigate this once in a lifetime journey. So, cherish it, keep your Bible beside you as you read through the chapters and ponder on what lies ahead for you now and in eternity with your Father who brought you here.

The inspiration for the title and to write this book came from the Holy Spirit who knows our hearts. The encouragement stems from writing my twice monthly devotionals for different people all over the world and from the lessons I learned living for God from my tender years through struggles and challenges. I learned to trade my struggles and challenges for the grace, mercy and strength of my Creator. I also gradually gained His perspective in difficult situations and challenges. Jesus' assurance that I am the light of the world (John 8:12b), encouraged and still encourages me in my walk with God. He is a miracle working God ! He is a miracle working Father ! He is the Alpha and Omega ! He is a miracle working God ! Yes God, I am a walking miracle and a living witness that God is alive and working on planet earth. Thank You God for giving me this opportunity. God, may my life be a continuous song of praise to You for as long as I live. Amen.

Some of the ideas in the book also come from preparation in writing those devotionals over the last four years and from daily readings of the Word of God. I have also been spiritually inspired and encouraged by reading Our Daily Bread, United Christian Broadcasting/Word for Today, Encouragement for Today of Proverbs 31 Ministries and Every Day With Jesus daily devotionals over the years and perusing Oswald Chambers' Utmost Classic Readings and Prayers daily.

Acknowledgements

Firstly, I want to thank God: The Creator of the Universe and the Giver of life for giving me the inspiration and ideas to write this book. Thank you, God for your sustenance, protection and help over the years. Secondly, I want to thank all those that stood by and encouraged me while I completed this book.

Who is Mary Olufunmilayo Adekson ?

My childhood was full of spiritual adventures after I accepted the Lord Jesus Christ as my Lord and Savior when I was 8 years old. My life has not been the same ever since I encountered my Lord. I remember clinging tightly to the beautiful picture of the lilies (Matthew 6:28-30) that my Sunday School Teacher gave us after her sermon to us about God's provision and care, that unforgettable and divine Sunday. I determined and resolved in my heart to love this Almighty Father who takes care of the lilies in the field which are here today and destroyed tomorrow. I possessed a child-like belief that this God is going to take care of me throughout my life here on earth. The rest is history. I was transformed with a dramatic vision of God with a personal relationship with Him and God has proved Himself to me over all these years and He still continues to deliver on His Promises. I go to Him for answers for all situations in my life. He listens and answers my cries, petitions and prayers. I am also grateful to my Godly earthly father, late Papa Gabriel Omodele Ekundiya Asanbe-Williams who stood by me during trials, troubles and tribulations. As Psalm 112 verse 6b says, "The righteous shall be in everlasting remembrance." You are remembered for all your fatherly care for me and my family.

I am a walking miracle because of Jesus Christ who loves me. I am grateful to You God for the opportunity to know You and be a living witness for You. I stand ! I stand in awe of You !! Holy God to whom all praise is due !!! I stand in awe of You !!!! Thank you so much God. You are AWESOME and GREAT !!!!!

Introduction

Poet C. T. Studd wrote: "Only one life, twill soon be past, only what's done for Christ will last."

We all wake up every day with plans about what will transpire in our lives for that particular day. The Westminster Confession of Faith says, "The chief end of man is that he might glorify God." Have you ever thought about your life and the Creator, Giver and Preserver of life? God is only a breath away if you acknowledge Him. Some of us say some prayers, read the Word before we venture out into the world. While some just whisper some words and go our way. When we acknowledge God for who He is in our lives as we move around including when we start our days, He acknowledges and protects us from the whims and caprices of the evil one and its cohorts.

I have set the Lord always before me because He is at my right hand I shall never be moved (Psalm 16:8). I will bless the Lord at all times and His praise shall continually be in my mouth (Psalm 34:1). Wouldn't it be Godly and encouraging if we set some time to talk to Our Father, ask Him for guidance and protection before we rush out the door each day? It's something to ruminate and pray about and also start practicing until it becomes our habits. Afterall, we give precious and special times to other people in our lives intimately from time to time. Why not give some few minutes (30 minutes or so) to talk to your Creator before venturing into the unknown world every morning? Just a suggestion.

Run to God: Find solace in God every morning before you leave home because "the name of the Lord is a strong tower; the righteous run to it, and are safe" (Proverbs 18:10). So, let your whole life be rooted and grounded in God because you only live once, so live for your Creator, Almighty God.

CHAPTER 1

Don't be unequally yoked with unbelievers

Some of the problems we encounter as born-again Christians stem from being unequally yoked with unbelievers. God warned us in His Word not to be unequally yoked with unbelievers. "Do not be unequally yoked together with unbelievers. For what fellowship has righteousness with lawlessness. And what communion has light with darkness? And what accord has Christ with Belial? Or what part has a believer with an unbeliever? And what agreement has the temple of God with idols?" (2 Corinthians 6:14-16). James said in chapter 4 verse 4 that, "do you not know that friendship with the world is enmity with God? Whoever therefore wants to be a friend of the world makes himself an enemy of God. Or do you think that the Scripture says in vain, the Spirit who dwells in us yearns jealously." This means we must steer clear of entering into relationships in different areas like dating, marriage and business to name a few, with unbelievers. Before you venture into any relationship, pray, fast, ask God and ask the Holy Spirit to lead you into the right relationship. Afterall, God says in His Word that if anyone lacks wisdom let her or him ask from God (James 1:5). But before you pray make sure the person you are praying about is a born-again Christian. If the person is not saved and is not a "genuine" child of God, run and keep clear of the relationship. Do not use any excuse like he or she will be saved after I enter into alliance or relationship with her or him. So many born-again Christians have lost their places in the kingdom because of being unequally yoked. So, do not be enticed or deceived because whatsoever a man or woman sows he or she shall reap (Galatians 6:7). And reap them you will with your problems related to raising your off-springs alone or with a spouse who is an unbeliever, if it is a marriage alliance or with diluted business dealings, if it is a business alliance. It is wise not to enter into the alliance in the first place than to live with regret and remorse for the rest of your just this one-given life. So beware, my sisters and brothers, live this your one life for God who created you in His image.

God instructed the Israelites not to intermarry with godless nations around them when they entered the promised land. He had an excellent reason for giving this instruction. If we as Christians marry or have a relationship with an ungodly person we are bound to be influenced by his or her ways and beliefs. There is no way you can walk or have a relationship with someone over a period of time that they will not influence your thoughts, actions and behaviors. So, beware, look, listen and pray. Do not cross that line, because once you cross it, it will be difficult to backtrack. The relationship is bound to leave more than a sour taste in your mouth. It will not only affect your mind, but it will also impede your spiritual growth because, can two walk together unless they agree? (Amos 3:3) If you fail to agree, there will be rancor and fights. This will eventually lead to further sufferings and biting of the tongue.

If you are heading in a direction, and your mother or father or both of them alert you to some obstacles or they inform you of some difficulties they observe in your relationship, halt, pray, heed and seek their spiritual advice. If you are obstinate or fail to heed Godly advice or harden your heart (Psalm 95:8), you are likely to end up in a disastrous outcome because fools despise wisdom and instruction (Proverbs 1:7). Let the fear of the Lord and the advice of your elders allow you to be cautious when entering wicked and ungodly relationships (Proverbs 4:14-17). Note that your parents speak objectively from experience and the wisdom that is from God and the Word of God. Proverbs 3 verse 7 cautions you not to be wise in your own eyes. Cautiously beware of entering into any relationship that will lead to anguish and unwarranted sufferings. Let discretion preserve you and let understanding keep you safe (Proverbs 2:11) and let the Lord direct your paths (Proverbs 3:6).

CHAPTER 2

Although there will be obstacles. God is faithful.

God proves Himself faithful to us as His children all the time even when we are not perfect which is most of the time. God has chosen you like the Israelites as his chosen people (Deuteronomy 7:9; 1 Peter 2:9-10). Since we are His chosen generation and people, we have Jesus Christ's promises etched out for us in our lives and in the lives of those in our households that cannot fail. God who identifies us with His Son when we accept Him as Our Lord and Savior, will always stick with us through thick or thin and help us avoid sin and temptations through the help of the Holy Spirit (Matthew 6:13). Be led by the Holy Spirit and say no to your carnal nature because "the Christian life is one of spiritual courage and determination lived out in our flesh" (Oswald Chambers). Remember, we can do all things through Jesus Christ who strengthens us

(Philippians 4:13). Rely on God: the unshakeable and unchanging One.

One thing that is very difficult for us as human beings is the acceptance of suffering as part of our human condition. Get the right perspective on suffering. Look upward to God for solace because God knows what it is like to experience pain because He watched His only son as He was nailed to the cross. So, share your feelings of pain and disillusionment with Your Father. He will make all grace abound towards you. God, who knows the end from the beginning knows how everything will end and He brings good things out of bad experiences. He loves you and knows and perceives all things and He will do what is best for you. Obey and get His blessings because you can do all things through Jesus Christ who strengthens you (Philippians 4:13). Obedience is powerful. It leads to God's blessings because to obey is better than sacrifice (1 Samuel 15:22). He will give you the power and grace to endure and ultimately make all things work together for good for you (Romans 8:28). You will have cause to glorify His Name. His timing, location and purpose will always be on target for your life. Do not focus on your circumstances or what you see because the hands that control the universe are wise, loving and compassionate. We can trust these hands in spite of our circumstances and not fear. God, the Master of Creation, the Universe, the world, our homes, our lives will sustain us and see us through. Our weakness is a blessing when we lean on God's power and strength. Pray Jehoshaphat's prayer to God in 2 Chronicles 20 verse 12b that says Lord "we do not know what to do but our eyes are on you."

Pray to perceive what God sees about your sufferings and the outcome for a better relationship with Him. Joanie Yoder of Our Daily Bread Ministries reiterated that, "God chooses what we go through; we choose how we go through it." So, trust God and lean on His power and direction to lead you through trials and sufferings. His power will be made manifest in your life. And as God assured Moses in Exodus 33 verse 14, pray that His presence remains with you throughout your time here on earth. Since we are hidden in the cleft of His Hands and in the shadow of His wings (Exodus 33:22; Psalm 17:8), let us remain securely under His everlasting arms (Deuteronomy 33:27). It is important to know that if we wait fervently and patiently on the Lord for whatever we are hoping for, God will redeem and give us justice (Psalm 27:14). God is all-sufficient. Trust in His goodness, character, justice, love, grace, mercy, wisdom and victory. "For the Lord will go before you. And the God of Israel will be your rear guard" (Isaiah 52:12c). Also be assured that "the Lord your God is with you wherever you go" (Joshua 1:9c). And be assured of his forgiveness, healing, protection and deliverance. Be assured of one thing, God will never forget you (Isaiah 49:14-15). He inscribed us on the palms of His Hands (Isaiah 49:16). This promise is ours when we put all our trust and faith in Him and in His goodness. Because God's promises never fail, they are new every morning. Great is His faithfulness (Lamentations 3:22-23). John Piper reiterates that, "there is no power in the universe that can stop God from fulfilling His totally good plans for you." God's excellent plans for your life will prevail. He is always working in your favor all the time whatever the circumstance. Jesus assures us through His word in John 16 verse 33 that, "in the world you will have tribulation; but be of good cheer, I have overcome the world." Because you are God's chosen people you have overcome the world. He has overcome the world and we have overcome the world because we are His children, the apple of His eye, the crown of creation, His friend and beloved. We are joint heirs with Jesus Christ who possesses the power and authority to calm the storms in our lives. We can do all things through Jesus Christ who strengthens us (Philippians 4:13). Our difficulties are there to glorify God. God has a plan to accomplish His will in our lives. God wants to turn the messes in our lives to messages that will bring more to the throne of grace and adore God as Almighty. You are more than conquerors through Jesus Christ who loves you (Romans 8:37). Since we seek and trust in the Lord "we shall not lack any good thing" (Psalm 34:10b) because greater is He that is in us than he (the devil) that is in the world (1 John 4:4). Our Almighty Father protects, provides, directs and fights for His children every moment of the day. Our God is awesome! Wait patiently for Him because He never fails and He is faithful. David, a man after God's heart, saw God as a rock, deliverer, protector, shield, refuge, friend, deliverer and he was very mindful of the God who can keep him safe (Psalm 18; 2 Samuel 22). Like Job, let our unshakeable God be the source of all meaning and permanence in our lives (Job 42:1-6). Hannah was an excellent example of one who based her faith on what she knew about her God, that He will always be faithful whatever her circumstances (1 Samuel 1). In due time, God came true for Hannah. She conceived and bore Samuel and even more children. When we put our total trust and faith in God, supernatural things happen in our lives (Proverbs 29:18). "You can be confident about tomorrow if you walk with God today" (David C. McCasland, Our Daily Bread Ministries). Our God is enough and even more than enough for us !

Suffering is part of life. Your suffering will make you mature in Christ and His Word (Psalm 9:12 & 1-20; Isaiah 49:13-18; James 5:10-11). Job asserted in Chapter 5 verse 7, that "but as for me, I would seek God. And to God I would commit my cause." Because, "many are the afflictions of the righteous but the Lord delivers him out of them all. He guards all his bones; not one of them is broken" (Psalm 34:19-20). Let God turn your obstacles and struggles into strengths (Hebrews 11:34 & 30-40) as He did with men and women in the Old and New Testament. Learn to follow God through obedience as you navigate trials, difficulties that you do not understand. God uses your difficult journeys to teach you patience, refine your character and make you ready for greater challenges and work in His vineyard. Allow God to turn your negative experiences into positives (Proverbs 24:16). Ernest Hemmingway supported this fact in "A Farewell to Arms" by saying that although the world breaks everyone, many are strong at the broken places and they are able to recover from the brokenness to become stronger. God encourages us that He will instruct us and teach us in the way we should go (Psalm 32:8). So, hang in there. Persevere. Endure. God will make your life a spectacle of success like He did for Job and Joseph and it will be well with you and your soul. He will not test us beyond what we can bear (James 1:2-4). He loves us too much to leave us in suffering for too long. God lovingly allows us to go through suffering so we can learn to trust Him and also have a testimony (Isaiah 43:2; 1 Thessalonians 3:2 & 3). So, seek to walk with joy, praise and victory in the midst of the most difficult situations, obstacles and sufferings. Oswald Chambers points out that "a saint doesn't know the joy of the Lord in spite of tribulation, but because of it"(2 Corinthians 7:4). C. S Lewis asserted that, "affliction is often that thing which prepares an ordinary person for some sort of an extraordinary destiny." Paul assured those that were with him on his journey that he trusts God because it will just be exactly as He has told him (Acts 27:23-25). You need to believe and trust God too that it will just be exactly as God has promised you. Let your faith in Your Father's plan and protection for you be greater than what might happen through your sufferings. Draw on God's redemptive grace for strength to become an extraordinary and patient child of God because all things work together for good for those that love God and He shall perfect all that belongs to you (Romans 8:28; Psalm 138:8a; Genesis 45:1-8; Psalm 62:1-4; & 11-12). Remember from the story of Job and other children of God, that God can be trusted. I, as the writer of this piece con-firms from my personal experience with Our Almighty Father, that He can be trusted. All we need to do is follow His lead and heed in obedience (Psalm 118:8-9). God ultimately transforms us into His master-pieces and He allows the fruit of the Spirit to become manifested in our lives (Galatians 5:22-23). Our growth in faith is made possible through our abilities to endure and overcome sufferings, difficulties and obstacles. "When we have nothing left but God, we'll find that God is enough" (Vernon C. Grounds, Our Daily Bread Ministries).

Have a repentant and contrite heart. When you commit a sin or sins ask God for forgiveness like David did (Psalms 32 & 51). He will forgive you because of the blood of Jesus Christ. Our hidden and dynamite weapon which prevents us from temptations are memorized Scriptures as needed topics. Holy Spirit brings them to mind when we face temptation as He did for Jesus in Matthew 4. God speaks to us in simple, ordinary and direct ways. "Likewise, the Spirit also helps us in our weaknesses. For we do not know what we should pray for as we ought, but the Spirit Himself makes intercessions for us with groaning which cannot be uttered. Now, He who searches the hearts knows what the mind of the Spirit is because He makes intercession for the saints according to the will of God" (Romans 8:26-27). The Spirit equips us to know what God is saying to us and also encourages us to have an intimate walk and close relationship with God. Diligence and devotion both matter to Our Father. Hide God's Word in your heart so that you will not sin against God or go back to worldly ways (Psalm 119:11; Proverbs 1:10; 2 Corinthians 10:4; Titus 2:11-12; 1 Corinthians 10:13). Study the Word (Joshua 1:8). Meditate on the Word day and night to have divine and physical prosperity. God remains faithful even when things around us looks to be in the contrary and are unpredictable because the promises of God are Yes and Amen (2 Corinthians 1:20). God is constant and permanent, while we are prone to changes and inconsistencies. Remember, God is in control and in charge of our lives. He is the driver of our life's vehicles. Allow Him to take charge and you will have cause to glorify His Name throughout your life here on earth. There is nothing God cannot do. What He has done for others He will do for you. David Egner of Our Daily Bread Ministries reiterated that, "trusting God's faithfulness dispels our fearfulness" (fear, worry and doubt). God is available 24/7 to hold us by His strong Hand.

You must have a vision that is born of God. A vision that is in line with His Word and teaching that will make you to become a new creation in Jesus Christ (2 Corinthians 5:17-18). Surrender and be crucified with Christ and live daily with Him. Be overcomers of temptation through patience and your faith in Jesus Christ (James 1:3).

Our next weapon is prayer. Our Lord Jesus Christ used prayer earnestly during His time on earth. Every time we open our Bible in the Gospels, we read that He rose up early to a quiet place to pray (Mark 1:35). Jesus instructed us to watch and pray so we do not enter into temptation like Judas Iscariot did (Matthew 26:49). Paul admonishes us to pray in Ephesians 6 verse 18. Pray in the Spirit. Pray to God about your life and the well-being of your family and the devil will flee from you and your household. Pray in advance for victory, holiness and for a life pleasing to your Creator. Spend quality time reading your Bible and talking with and listening to God, the Author of your life. C. S. Lewis says that, "what is important to God is that we open ourselves to His love and pass on that love to others."

Obey God. Have a well prepared and obedience mindset. For to obey is better than sacrifice (1 Samuel 15:22; Philemon 21). Obey God's laws as laid down in Exodus 20. But we also have to listen to the Holy Spirit as He bids and directs us during struggles and obstacles that God brought about to strengthen and make us to become His faithful son and daughter like Joseph and Daniel. "If we are born of God we will see His guiding Hand (in everything) and give Him the credit" (Oswald Chambers). Stand on the promises that cannot fail.

The thing that matters most is our personal relationship with God. This relationship gives us the joy of the Lord which is our strength (Nehemiah 8:10). Knowing that God loves us relieves us from fear and allows us to cling to Our Heavenly Father and receive His blessings. And when you stumble, do not be afraid to come back to your Father. He is waiting for you as His prodigal son (Luke 15:20; Isaiah 41:13). You can start again because Our Father is the God of new beginnings. "Though the righteous fall seven times, they rise again (Proverbs 24:16a) but the wicked shall fall into mischief (Proverbs 24:16b). The same power that raised Jesus Christ Our Savior from the dead (Romans 8:11), gives you God-power that resides in you through the Holy Spirit, to begin again (Ephesians 3:20). Regardless of your situation today have hope in God through the promises of His Word that all shall be well because hope never disappoints (Romans 5:5). And the best place to be is at the center of Your Father's will. So have faith and do not fear. Our faithful Father is in total control of your life (Revelation 1:8 &17-18; Isaiah 44:6). Look up to Him as your Father and do not forget to be an obedient and faithful son and daughter. Come on, enjoy the blessings of your Father and do not look back because those who look back will not be fit for the Kingdom of Heaven (Luke 9:62). Our God is loyal, faithful, dependable, loving and painstaking. That is our Papa. God was faithful to Abraham, David, Moses, Elijah, Enoch, Elisha, Joseph, Daniel, Shadrach, Meshach and Abednego, to mention just a few and He will be faithful to you too. So, cling to the Father who will never fail or disappoint you.

God envelopes us with His love while we sift through guilt and regrets over those things, we wish we could undo. Jesus Christ draws us close with His divine redemptive power (1 John 3:19-24). There is therefore no condemnation to those that are in Christ Jesus (Romans 8:1). Our Papa is strong and faithful. In Matthew 6 verses 25 to 34 Jesus encouraged us to rely on God and not worry as all God's creation rely on Him for their existence, so you also will be securely taken care of. So, move forward into a future full of hope and prosperity and just be like the lilies and the birds of the air. Leave all your tomorrows in His Hands and walk by faith not by sight (2 Corinthians 5:7). God who names and holds each star in place will never forget or lose us. God who holds us under the shadow of His wings (Psalm 17:8), really loves us and knows our names. So, my dear, rely solely on God your Father who holds the promises that cannot fail on your behalf. Claim and stand on these promises. Our God who is faithful, will not fail you because He will neither leave you nor forsake you (Deuteronomy 31:8). He will fight for you and make you victorious. You are blessed because you hope in your Creator (Jeremiah 17:7-8). God is majestic, unlimited, infallible and He is Almighty. He is Omnipotent, Omnipresent and Omniscience. God rules and reigns with all might, power and authority (Isaiah 6:8, 40:14; Job 38:1-42). Do not perceive your problems, obstacles and sufferings as supreme. Keep your focus and gaze on the Almighty who brought you here for a purpose. Hudson Taylor, a British missionary to China in the late 1800s gave this advice: "the branch of the vine does not worry and toil, and rush here to seek for sunshine, and there to find rain. No, it rests in union and communion with the vine; and at the right time, and in the right way, is the right fruit found on it." Let us therefore abide in the Lord Jesus Christ because if we do and His Word abide in us we shall bear fruits in due season. Act, by abiding, trusting with faith and waiting. God is always with us to guide, strengthen and comfort us every time. Teach us to lean on you Lord because trusting in Your faithfulness can dispel our fears (Isaiah 25:1-9). When you walk with God, you can count on Him to protect you (Daniel 6). God does not only protect you, He provides for you, heals you, directs your paths, showers you with grace and mercy and also loves and cares for you.

CHAPTER 3

Grow up wise.

Solomon, the wisest man that lived informed us that wisdom is the cornerstone of Christian living. He admonishes us that the fear of the Lord is the beginning of wisdom (Proverbs 1:7; Proverbs 15:33a). Because "the wisdom that is from above is first pure, then peaceable, gentle, willing to yield, full of mercy and good fruits, without partiality and without hypocrisy" (James 3:17). The Word says in Proverbs 28 verse 26 that, "He who trusts in his own heart is a fool. But whoever walks wisely will be delivered." "A man's heart plans his way, but the Lord directs his steps" (Proverbs 16:9). Most mature born-again Christians will agree that seeking and embracing wisdom prevents them from making self-destructive foolish mistakes and allows them to live a long wisely inspired life as a child of God. Live wisely and not foolishly like the ungodly. Let God lead you throughout your life and in all your life's pursuits. Avoid living careless, foolish lives. Because a life of purpose is more rewarding than gaining popularity or power. Peruse the

Word of God for the right Christlike way to live so that you do not go astray like the prodigal. And when you realize you do or are moving away from Him, redirect and refocus. Cry out and He will come to your rescue. He is Our Rock and Redeemer. Your Heavenly Father is always waiting in love to get you back on track. God is concerned, He hears, He sees, and He rescues His children from the whims and caprices of the evil one and worldly enticements. Remember you are never out of God's reach. He watches over you and send His angels to protect you 24/7. Choose God and let God give you His best. Do not forget to spend time wisely. Don't just spend time anyhow, invest time wisely every moment. Work hard. And don't be a sluggard (Proverbs 6:6-9; 24:30-31; 10:26).

James encourages us in James 1 verse 5 that if any of us lack wisdom we should ask from God who gives liberally. Solomon asked for wisdom and he got more blessings than he bargained for. He got wealth and fame. That is the reward from the God we serve. If we have Godly-wisdom we will have the discretion and discernment to navigate the obstacles and sufferings of life with courage and God's guidance because our God is greater than all of our troubles (Psalm 93:1 & Ephesians 3:20). He can do exceedingly above what we ask or think. As Oswald Chambers said: "Some extraordinary thing happens to someone who hold on to the love of God when the odds are totally against him (or her)." And A.W. Tozer reiterated that: "wisdom is always associated with righteousness and humility and is never found apart from godliness and true holiness."

Remember: God has given you this one life and opportunity. Avoid rushing into intimate relationship self destructively, foolishly and carelessly. Pray, talk to God. Seek wise and Godly counsel and pray fervently to avoid making self-defeating foolish decisions and consequential mistakes. Paul encourages us to "also aspire to lead a quiet life" (1 Thessalonians 4:11). Paul instructs us further in Ephesians 5:15 to "see that you walk circumspectly, not as fools but as wise, redeeming the time, because the days are evil." Paul further instructs us in Ephesians 5 verse 16, to know what the will of the Lord is as a wise person. Keep yourself pure until marriage. And when you get married be committed to your mate in holy union for life.

Be humble, and listen to wise Godly advice from respectful and experienced children of God. Respect your parents and elders in the Lord. Trouble, challenges and disappointments will surely come, but when you throw yourself on God's mercy, love, care and direction, and use wise discernment and discretion you will overcome because our Lord is bigger than all our problems, challenges, troubles and disappointments.

As a born-again child of God do not give way to anger in your lives because "he who is slow to anger is better than the mighty. And he who rules his spirit than he who takes a city" (Proverbs 16:32). So be cautious when you are prone to anger, pray to God to help you disband your angry spirit. The word 'anger' is only one letter short of the word 'danger'. So, ask God to help you manage your anger because a quick-tempered man acts foolishly (Proverbs 14:17). Anger brings shame and destroys lives and relationships. Be closer to God and He will be closer to you and help you through constant prayers and self-control to combat anger. Pray constantly for calmness, the fruits of the Spirit (Galatians 5:22-23) and God's peace, and practice self-discipline all the time. Think positively and in line with the Word of God. As you think so are you. A man of knowledge uses word with restraint (Proverbs 17:27). Pray that God give you an even-tempered spirit.

Words of God enriches and satisfies your soul and is also beneficial to your body and mind. Know that you belong to God. Your identity is hidden in Jesus Christ. So do not let anyone deceive you that you have no identity or that you need any new identity. Acknowledge God's greatness and power. Choose your words wisely and with humility of heart carefully weighing how your words affect those around you. Remember, our words are a recognition of who we are as God's ambassadors and children. Let the promises of God to you in His Word be the landmark of your life and actions. Ralph Waldo Emerson said, "sow a thought and you reap an action; sow an act and you reap a habit; sow a habit and you reap a character and you reap a destiny." Be full of God's grace and character as you peruse His Word and chew on them as honey. Let God write His new Name in your life. When God does this, pride, self-interest and self-sufficiency will be completely erased from your life and Jesus will be everything to you.

Do not follow in the counsel of the wicked because "there is a way that seems right to a man. But the end is the way of death" (Proverbs 16:25). If we have the right perspective toward God and let our reliance be on Him, everything in our lives will fall into their proper places. "Yielding to Jesus will break every kind of slavery in (that) person's life" (Oswald Chambers).

CHAPTER 4

Be prayerful. Fast when you can. Pray in the Spirit always.

Prayer is the cornerstone of Christian-living. John Wesley reiterated that, "God does nothing redemptively in this world except by prayer." On several occasions during His earthly ministry, Our Lord Jesus Christ went out to solitary places to pray. Mark recorded that, "now in the morning having risen a long while before daylight, He went out and departed to a solitary place; and there He prayed (Mark 1:35). If Jesus Christ communed with His Father before embarking on a mission, what is stopping us from doing the same. We should seek the Lord early. Jesus was able to cope with the demands of his human nature by spending time alone with God. Spend time alone with God and experience His strength, energy, fulfilment, protection, victory and security. "The closer we walk with God, the clearer we see His guidance" (Joe Stowell, Our Daily Bread Ministries). As the psalmist proclaims, "O God You are my God. Early will I seek You" (Psalm 63:1). God's faithfulness, love and compassion are new every morning (Lamentations 3:22-23). Jonah said, "when my soul fainted within me, I remembered the Lord; And my prayer went up to You, into Your holy temple" (Jonah 2:7). Micah reiterated that, "therefore I will look to the Lord; I will wait for the God of my salvation; my God will hear me" (Micah 7:7). "Ask and it will be given to you, seek, and you will find, knock, and it will be opened to you. For everyone who asks receives, and he who seeks finds, and to him who knocks it will be opened" (Matthew 7:7-8; Luke 11:9-10). And Jesus said, "again I say to you that if two of you agree on earth concerning anything that they ask, it will be done for them by My Father in heaven. For where two or three are gathered together in My name, I am there in the midst of them" (Matthew 18:19-20). So, Jesus also said, "and whatever things you ask in prayer, believing, you will receive" (Matthew 21:22). Jesus continued, "therefore I say to you whatever things you ask when you pray, believe that you receive them and you will have them" (Mark 11:24; John 14:13-14; John15:7; John16:23-24). Our Father wants to hear from us, and He also wants us to listen to Him. We can do this through daily and persistent prayer asking in Jesus' Name. For the effective fervent prayer of the righteous man (and woman) avails much (James 5:16b). For prayer to be effective it should flow from a trusting and persevering heart. That is, a heart that believes and knows that all things will work together for his or her good. When we trust and bless the Lord, He blesses us abundantly. Be dependent on God physically and spiritually. It is excellent that we continue to ask, because God honors our requests and this increases our gratitude to Him. So, to be anxious about nothing, pray about everything (Philippians 4:6) and depend on God for everything. Infinitely Holy God who is limitless and who holds the universe in His Hands, cares that our needs are met and He will ensure that His will is manifested in our lives. Let your thoughts, actions, words and prayers align with God 's Word. Meditate, talk to God and listen to His directions. Have an intimate loving relationship with the God of the universe through your warmth, passion, praise, expressions of gratitude to Him for His love, mercy, grace, provision, joy, surprise blessings and victory. As I pointed out earlier, God is in the business of answering prayers (Matthew 21:22) according to His riches in glory to be in line with His will. Our prayers are like incense and sacrifice to God (Psalm 141:2; Exodus 30:7-8). As Jesus Christ taught us to pray: God will give us this day our daily bread (Matthew 6:11). Cast all your cares on God and you will have peace because God keeps those who trust in Him in perfect peace (Isaiah 26:3). God will not withhold any good thing from His children who walk uprightly (Psalm 84:11).

Pray to God to give you your prayer language that you can use to pray in the Spirit. Use this language to intimately pray at least 15 minutes a day. Fast when you can as a buttress to your prayers. If your health does not allow you to, God understands. Ask for the assistance of genuine prayer warriors when you need it. They can agree with you in your battle through genuine and warriorlike prayers and be along your side as you win the battle. As Jesus Christ interceded and mediated on our behalf we should also intervene on behalf of others. Our prayers are precious to God. When we call, He answers. "Behold the Lord's hand is not shortened that it cannot save nor his ear heavy that it cannot hear" (Isaiah 59:1). Draw near to God and He will draw near to you (James 4:8). God's eyes are upon the righteous and His ears are open to their cries (Psalm 34:15; 1 Peter 3:12).

Listen to God (Psalm 32:8; Isaiah 30:12). Allow the Holy Spirit to lead you every second of the day. Let the Holy Spirit guide you (Galatians 5:16). When the Holy Spirit lives in you it affects every area of your life. Follow His leads because He is our eternal guide. When the Holy Spirit tugs your heart about something or the path you are following, listen and take action immediately. Do not hesitate. He is there for a spiritual reason: to direct your paths from destructive tendencies, actions and behaviors. Holy Spirit teaches us to walk with God through constant reminding (John 14:26). Nowadays God speaks to us through the Holy Spirit and through His Word in the Holy Bible. To hear Him we should be willing to be still and say like Samuel: "Speak for your servant is listening" (1 Samuel 3:10). We need to be open, sensitive and receptive to His Voice because "if we live in the Spirit let us also walk in the Spirit" (Galatians 5:25). Lean not on your own understanding and acknowledge Him in all your ways and let Him direct your paths to productive and Spiritual well-being and wholeness. We need divine guidance in our journey through life while we are here. Leave the driving of your life to God. Let God take charge and also let Him take control. Holy Spirit supplies us with the ability to perceive what God is saying and He also helps us to develop a closer relationship with God and see God clearly as He is. Spiritual growth comes about through the power of the Holy Spirit as we submit to His maturing process. The Spirit lives inside us as believers to refresh and renew us.

Pray that God's kingdom come and that His will be done on earth as it is done in heaven (Matthew 6:10). God, who makes missed opportunities to become great miracles, will hear your cries because when we pray and cry to Him, He listens and answers our pleas. God will clothe us with righteousness, love, prosperity and victory. God who is the God of impossibility will answer your cries as He did for Abraham and Sarah, for Shadrach, Meshach and Abednego (Genesis 18:12; Daniel 3). Daniel through his act of prayer, showed us not to panic in the face of obstacles and problems that we cannot control (Daniel 6:1-15). Believe God for all things that seem impossible (John 11:25-26; Jeremiah 32:17 & 27; Luke 18:27) because nothing is too hard for Our Father. Our Miracle working Father will answer all your cries, petitions, and entreaties. When you pray incessantly for all your needs and other people's needs you become a prayer warrior and subsequently a walking miracle. God endows your ordinariness to become extraordinary. When we surrender to God's will come what may, as someone has said, "the hallelujah of triumph is louder than the Amen of resignation." If we can cultivate an attitude of triumph in the face of sorrow, loss, disappointment, disaster, disillusionment, frustration, suffering and bereavement and recline on God's will, our spirit will be victorious and we will have a winning attitude. Prayer invites God to do what you cannot do. So, invite God into your life, pray without ceasing. Nehemiah prayed (Nehemiah 1:11) waited, and trusted God for success and acted on what God told him to do because he knows that we are not capable of managing our own affairs without God's continuous help. If we constantly cultivate the habit of prayer, our Father through his will, will supply our needs according to His riches in glory in Christ Jesus (Philippians 4:19). Wait patiently for God's answers and know that delay from God is not denial. So, do not worry but pray and wait, and thank God for answers to your prayers (Philippians 4:6). Turn every worry to prayer. Leave your worries at the foot of the cross and do not take them back because you cannot change anything by worrying. Why worry when you can pray. Trust in Jesus He is the Way. Mart DeHaan II admonished us that, "he or (she) who abandons himself or (herself) to God will never be abandoned by God" (Mart DeHaan II, Our Daily Bread Ministries). So, pray for God's will to be manifest in your life. God's will, will be done on earth as it is in heaven (Matthew 6:10). God's ways and thoughts are higher than ours and his wisdom is beyond what we mere humans can comprehend. God can be trusted because He is faithful and just in all His ways. So, ensure that you seek God's face for every area of your life. His past faithfulness should always remind us that His faithfulness will endure forever. To record and put the fulfilment of His promises in our lives for answered prayers, we should keep a journal. Record your prayers and thank Him when the prayers you offered have been answered. Know your God pretty well and hope in Him with all confidence.

Be aware of the fact that the weapons of our warfare are not carnal but mighty in God for the pulling down of strongholds (2 Corinthians 10:4). Daniel prayed and reaped the effects of his prayers (Daniel 6). Prayer grows us to become reliant on God and it is the soil in which hope and healing grow best (James 5:16). Prayer invokes God's supernatural power into our lives and into our day to day affairs. Remember, His grace is sufficient for us (2 Corinthians 12:9). Draw near to God's grace through prayer and your spiritual enemy will run away from you (Ephesians 6:15-17 & 6:18; 1 Peter 5:8-9) and cast your burdens and worries on the Lord (1 Peter 5:7) for He cares for you. Leave what you do not know and what baffles you and make you shudder to the All-Knowing God, the Creator of the Universe. He is listening when we bend our knees or bow our heads to pray, His ears are wide open 24/7. "In repentance and rest is your salvation, in quietness and confidence shall be your strength" (Isaiah 30:15). Learn to be still before your Father. Attend to Him, read His Word and meditate on His Word and worship Him daily. Worship Him in truth and in the Spirit (John 4:24; 1 Corinthians 3:1-11; Ephesians 2 :19-20). When you live a life that continues on a Christlike path constant with the will of God, Heaven will smile on you. God will answer your prayers according to His wisdom by accomplishing what is best for you. All you have to do is pray as if everything depends on God; and work as if everything depends on you (2 Samuel 7:22) because our God is larger than all the problems we bring to Him. Trust God even when the journey is wild and scary. The people God used as examples in the Bible were not necessarily any braver, wiser, or smarter than us, they were just people with tenacity of purpose with unwavering faith who refused to take no for an answer (Hebrews 4:16; Hebrews 11). They kept on going and never looked back.

CHAPTER 5

Be genuine like Jesus Christ. Don't be fake.

Jesus showed us while on earth that genuineness is key. Jesus was Himself all the time. He valued Himself and others and He showed this trait in His interactions with all the people He came in contact with. In Jesus, what you see is what you got and still get. He said it as it is, using the Word of God. We should be like Jesus Christ as Christians because Jesus Christ pave the way for us to know God in reality. Jesus came down to earth, became one of us so we might become like Himself. Paul referred to Jesus Christ as "the image of the invisible God" (Colossians 1:15-17). This is saying that Jesus is God--- the Creator and Sustainer of all that God has made. One thing that we should not forget is that Jesus was also human because He came to dwell among us as Immanuel through Mary's womb with authority, forgiveness and superiority (Luke 4:18). He came to reconcile us to God (Colossians 1:20-22) and redeem us. Jesus Christ is the light of the world that radiates love, joy, peace, righteousness, truth, morality and justice. "Christ's victory in the past gives courage for the present and hope for the future" (Joe Stowell, Our Daily Bread Ministries). Pray that the Holy Spirit should inspire and assist you to be like Our Lord Jesus Christ. Jesus gives strength to the weak. He witnessed, healed and made Himself available to the poor and downtrodden as well as to the rich. He did not pretend or hide under any façade. Christ went about doing good while He walked on earth. Jesus' attitude won people over every time when He was on earth. He took the form of a servant and even washed His disciples' feet (John 13). So, we should humbly walk the earth, do good to all and be genuine and be transformed into the likeness of Christ (2 Corinthians 3:18). Let us be like Jesus Christ who laid down His life for us and lived here on earth serving others. Try to be genuine as you help others. Do the works that Jesus did because He informed us that those who believe in Him the works that He did we will also do (John 14:12) and greater works will we do. What works did Jesus do on earth? He healed, He comforted, He loved, He taught, He encouraged, He gave life to the dead, and He blessed. These and whatever our hands find to do to glorify God's Name are what we should do (Ecclesiastes 9:10a; Romans 12:11 and Colossians 3:23). Produce Christ-like fruits (Galatians 5:22-23). Let the world know that you belong to Jesus through your kindness, joy and compassion. The Name of Jesus heals our wounds, drives away our fears and calms our sorrows. His Name oozes out salvation, freedom, healing, abundant joy, deliverance and love.

Jesus is an example of someone who walks in servanthood. His servanthood attitude can gracefully give us the strength to serve others while we are here on earth (Galatians 6:9; 2 Corinthians 10:9). Jesus said in Matthew 20 verse 26 that whosoever wants to be great in the kingdom should have the mindset and be willing to become a servant to those he or she serves. Jesus knew hunger and weariness and He shared everything of our human nature except sin. He came as a humble one and to the other Galileans, although Jesus looked ordinary to all, He was extraordinary. God therefore humbled Himself in His debut on earth to save us. So, we must do the same as we profess our faith before others. Let Jesus make you to become extraordinary like Himself (John 1:24-34). Jesus found strength in surrendering to His Father. Let us pray to the Father to give us a surrendering, gentle and obedient heart like His Son's. Emulate Jesus Christ. Be like Him. Have the mind of Christ in your dealings and interactions with different individuals. Jesus Christ was obedient to God during His abode on earth. Speak the truth in love. Make it a habit not to lie to anyone about anything. Let truth be the pillar of your life in all dealings as you perform your duties and use your talents to glorify your Father.

Jesus did not condone evil. That was why He taught us in the Lord's Prayer that we not be led into temptation but to be delivered from evil. Evil is the word "live" spelt backwards. Therefore "evil" could then be classified to be "anti life." So keep away from evil and live a wholly God-inspired transformed life as Jesus Our Savior did. Hate evil. Abhor any form of evil by staying close to your Redeemer. Detest all that is evil as God's child and cling to all that is good (Romans 12:9). Honest people should ensure that they speak out against evil and wickedness when they are perpetuated around them.

Jesus Christ was well-versed in the Word of God that he quoted them to the powers that be and to satan in His days. They marveled at His knowledge of the Scriptures even when he was still at a tender age. Be versed in the Word of God as God's child. Meditate on the Word. Lick His Word and let them be as honey in your mouth. God will prosper you if you read and meditate on His Word (Psalm 1:2; John 6:68; Job 23:12; Isaiah 55:11).

When you go through painful circumstances, whatever they are, remember Jesus Christ has been through it all: physical, relational, emotional. Jesus Christ walked this earth so He can identify with our sufferings. You have no excuse but to perceive what you are going through, through the lens of what Our Savior has been through. As the saying goes, remind yourself all the time: "what will Jesus do" and how will He see what I am going through in the light of all He was able to go through while on earth. The power of resurrection can make us do like Jesus do and be a genuine child of the King. Honor God in your relationships. Jesus Christ honor others and He respects all and sundry. It pleases Our Father when we honor others who are made in His image. Ensure that you do not do anything that will make others commit sins. Do not be a stumbling block to others as they travel on their journey to heaven (1 Corinthians 8:9-13). Be tenderhearted, compassionate and respectful as Jesus Christ was to the rich and the poor and those from diverse backgrounds.

CHAPTER 6

Focus on eternal life.

What is your destination? Have you ever thought about this? Do not live for temporal things that will perish. There have been so many sermons on the value of material things. But one Scripture passage sums it up: Seek ye first the kingdom of God and His righteousness and all other things will be added to you (Matthew 6:33). Do not store your treasures where moth will destroy them (Matthew 6:20). Store them in eternal store where they will not rust or be destroyed. Do not live like the rich fool in Luke 12 and "take heed and beware of coveteousness, for one's life does not consist in the abundance of the things he (or she) possesses" (Luke 12:15). Our relationship with Jesus Christ that stirs us up for eternal inheritance is something we cannot lose. Be rich in good deeds (1 Timothy 6:18) because our real treasure is not measured by all we have stored up here on earth, but in what we or with whom we spend our time, energy and passions. So, invest in those things that are eternal. Have a solid faith in Jesus Christ (James 2:5) and help and show others the way of salvation to Our Lord. Hold money, homes and earthly treasures loosely because you cannot take them with you. Look positively and encouragingly to store up eternal treasures by using your earthly treasures to glorify God's Name. Do not be like Achan in Joshua 7 verse 1, or like the rich young man in Matthew 19 verses 16 to 22 or like Ananias and Sapphira in Acts 5 verses 1 to 11. Live with the intention of facing God with smiles and "a well-done good and faithful servant" welcome greetings (Matthew 25:23), when you meet Him after your time here on earth is completed. The story of the beggar and the rich man that Jesus told His disciples in Luke 16 verses 22 to 23 and 27 to 28, vividly portrays the reality of heaven and hell. Serving Jesus means I no longer live for myself but live so the glory of God can be manifested in me and through me to others while I am here. Focus, dedicate your life and be disciplined as you serve Jesus (2 Corinthians 6:4-10; Hebrews 12 :2) because "those who are Christ's have crucified the flesh with its passions and desires" (Galatians 5:24) and they have inherited and embrace the joy of the Lord. When you accept Jesus Christ, you are joyful in spite of sufferings and challenges.

It is certain that the soul, which does not die, go to a place after we leave this earth. The souls of born-again Christians go to the Lord (1 Thessalonians 4:14). Live daily as a child of God bound for heaven. "For what will it profit a man (or woman) if he gains the whole world, and loses his own soul" (Mark 8:36).

Jesus Christ will come for those that are believers in Him and they will reign eternally with Him (1 Thessalonians 4:16-17). Because "precious in the sight of the Lord is the death of His saints" (Psalm 116:15). "The righteous shall be in everlasting remembrance" (Psalm 112:6b). The above facts from the Word of God gives us hope regarding eternal life and where we and our loved ones who believe in Jesus will spend eternity. Do not let anything detract you from living for God here. Pursue God's intended goals and live every second of each day with the intention of making it to Heaven because man is made to have a relationship with His Creator. There is always a vacuum left in our souls if we do not have a positive Christ-focused relationship with the Father. Oswald Chambers said that, "we have to ignore to the point of hatred anything that competes with our relationship to Him." We should be very attentive not to worship man made god and idols. God is jealous over us. This is why we should refrain from worshipping man-made gods. St. Augustine said, "you have made us for yourself, and our heart is restless until it rests in you." The 17th Century French Philosopher Blaise Pascal referred to these longing to be blessed and to acknowledge Our Maker as the "God-shaped hole." Pope Francis called it "nostalgia for God." Eternal life begins when we accept Jesus Christ as our Savior and do God's will everyday (John 17:3). "The Great in the kingdom have been those who.... love God more than others did" (A.W.Tozer). A. W. Tozer continued by adding that, "If your ambition is to have no ambition except to be pleasing to God, you are great in His kingdom." As ambassadors and strangers on earth, gaze and focus on your Creator and please Him with your words and actions because as Paul said, our current troubles are not worth the rewards that is to come (Romans 8:18).

Like Elijah said in 1 Kings 18 verse 21, choose who you want to worship :God of Israel or Baal? You also have a choice. Who do you want to worship: God or the devil with his lures of the world? Joshua told the Israelites that as for him and his house they will worship the Lord (Joshua 24:15c). Only the Almighty the maker of all human beings in His own image can fill the emptiness in human hearts. He is the one who can satisfy our souls and our thirsts for Spiritual water (John 4:14). Fix your eyes on Jesus. When I fix my eyes on Jesus, the things of the world will go faintly dim in the light of His grace "for one's life does not consist in the abundance of the things he (or she) possesses" (Luke 12:15c). Remember that only what is done for Jesus Christ will last. Let us therefore put everything we do now with our eternal destination in mind.

One thing is sure that the hour is coming when Jesus Christ will judge the dead and those that are alive (John 5:28-29). This is why you must be ready. Be bold, be strong, and be of good courage as you prepare yourself for that day. So, build your life on the Rock of Ages, the "I am that I am" and you will stand firm in this world and in the world to come with guaranteed eternal destiny. On Christ the solid rock we stand all other ground is sinking sand, all other ground is sinking sand. Father in heaven we recognize you as our sure foundation and security. May we know you now as our Savior rather than meet you in eternity as our judge. Amen

CHAPTER 7

Character matters.

We are not born with character. Character and integrity are not what we are all born with. We were all born in sin inherited from Adam. We develop character as we grow and through the blood of Jesus we were redeemed and reborn. So, we should imbibe Godly character into our youths through our exemplary lives and leading them in the Word of God from a tender age. In other words, it's not what we say alone but mostly what we do that helps aid in the development of character in our youths. This will allow our children to cultivate and inculcate Godly character within their hearts. Talking about and giving example of men like Joseph during discussions will help instill Godly character into our youths. The story of Joseph reveals that circumstances do not create character but reveal hidden character.

When I was growing up, my father always told me every morning before I ventured out into the world to "remember the daughter of who I am." I was always very cautious about the way I behaved when I remember this admonition. This advice spilled over into my life when I became a born-again Christian at eight years old. I always remind myself even until today, to remember the daughter of who I am. The daughter of Almighty God, the Creator of heaven and earth, who made me in His image. So, I implore you, as children of the Almighty to develop a Godly character and remember the son or daughter of who you are and walk in integrity all the time 24/7. You are very special and fearfully and wonderfully made (Psalm 139:14). Our values depend on God's love for us (Galatians 5:16-17). God has a heart of love, grace and mercy for us. So, remember to let your character showcase you to the world. This means you cannot steal, lie, cheat, gossip, deceive, manipulate, cut corners, or behave as those in the world behave in sight and out of sight. Don't compromise your integrity as a child of God. Be sincere. Be honest. Don't do what God abhors or detests. Don't relish among worldly ungodly friends. And as I wrote in the first chapter, don't be unequally yoked with unbelievers, always remember that your Heavenly Father is watching. And that as Paul said in Philippians 4 verse 8, "finally, brethren, whatsoever things are true, whatsoever things are honest, whatsoever things are just, whatsoever things are pure, whatsoever things are lovely, whatsoever things are of good report, if there be any praise, think on these things."

This reminds me of a story I read about a king who had no children. He thought out a plan for a successor to his throne. So, he called all his subjects to an assembly. He told the older ones to send him their children who were of school age. The king gave these children some seeds and informed each one of them that they should come back in a year with flower that sprout from the seeds. Everyone went home. After a year, the king called the assembly again. The young ones came with different sizes of flowers. The king looked at the flowers and said nothing. Then one lonely young boy came to the king with a bowl full of dirt. The young boy informed the king that he watered the seed so many times, but the seed never germinated. To the amazement and surprise of all his subjects at the assembly, the king said that the young lonely boy was going to be their next king because he was the only honest one among all the children. He said that the seeds he gave to all the children were dead seeds.

So, my dear brothers and sisters in the Lord, how honest are you when no one is watching? Honesty is the best policy. Character counts ! Integrity has it's reward !! So keep your integrity intact. Proverbs 10 verse 9 says, "He who walks with integrity walks securely, but he that perverts his ways will become known." "Remove falsehood and lies far from me" (Proverbs 30:8a). For further inspiration and wisdom read Titus 2:1-14. Let us be honest and walk in integrity because no liers or dishonest person will enter the kingdom of heaven (Revelation 21:8). Let us be ready to stand before our Heavenly Father blameless (Colossians 3:12 –13).

You can be stripped of your wealth, friends, fame, or even family, but not of your character and your faith in God. Eternal things will survive and outlast the temporal things on earth. So, honor God by the way you live as Abraham, Noah, Moses,

Job, Enoch and Joseph did. Joseph refused to sin even when that could have made him become a great man. And you see what happened. He got a better crown here on earth and in eternity with God (Genesis 39:16; 41:39-41). The only way to live a godly, holy, and undefeated life is to live life committed to the Lord. Since you only live once, develop a Godly character and make your life count for God. His love, peace, presence and security are the only things that can fill the voids in our lives. Let us understand that we should rely on You for our security, self-worth and significance. Endure, develop an inner strength of character based on personal integrity and have a deep inner conviction that you will face life with fortitude and integrity. You are to let your identity be in God, Whose you are, not on who you are. Everything He does, He does it well. Every move He makes, there's no mistake. He does all things well. He does all things well. Ruminate on and cultivate to have the fruit of the Spirit which is: "love, joy, peace, longsuffering, kindness, goodness, faithfulness, gentleness, self-control" (Galatians 5:22-23). Paul admonishes us not to "become conceited, provoking one another, envying one another" (Galatians 5:26). Let your lives reflect God's character which is loving, pure and holy.

Do not habor any evil thoughts in your hearts because your sin will find you out like it did with David and Saul the kings of Israel (2 Samuel 12; 1 Samuel 15) or it will haunt you as inner conflict or turmoil. Confess and work through any guilt you may have and pray to God to erase the stain of guilt from your heart (1 John 1 :7-10). Avoid greed so you do not end up like Judas Iscariot. The way you react to success or adversity can make or mar you. So be careful that you do not become vain and conceited or become totally dejected when either of this happens to you. "Give me neither poverty nor riches---Feed me with the food allotted to me. Lest I be full and deny You. And say who is the Lord? Or lest I be poor and steal, and profane the name of my God" (Proverbs 30:8-9). Be watchful for pride in your hearts as God prospers you. Be grateful for little and big blessings. Do not have a heart of envy, jealousy, anger or fighting within you as you interact with everyone God puts in your life.

Let your security be in Jesus Christ and His love and God's love for you, not on worldly things or people. Be content with whatever God has endowed you with. Paul said that he was always content in whatever situation he finds himself (Philippians 4:11). God, who is your shepherd will always provide you with all you need to live a victorious life and He will not let you want (Psalm 23). "And the Lord will make you the head and not the tail, you shall be above only, and not be beneath if you heed the commandments of the Lord your God which I command you today, and be careful to observe them" (Deuteronomy 28:13). Be careful not to give way to those who will kill the aspirations and dreams that God gives you. Be close to God. Seek His guidance and listen to the Holy Spirit's advice and proddings. God, who is excellent will make all things in your life work out for the best in the end (Lamentations 3:23-24; Psalm 116:1-9). Let the prayer of Augustine that entreats: "grant, Lord, that I may know myself as I know thee" God, be always close to your lips every day.

CHAPTER 8

Love genuinely.

Love your enemies. Pray for those who persecute and hate you. Joseph was a good example of God's child who told his brothers in Genesis 50 verse 20 that they meant evil against him but God turned it to good to save their lives and that of their children and grandchildren. "Hatred stirs up strife but love covers all sins" (Proverbs 10:12). First Corinthians 13 sums everything up, that love is supreme. If we can love, we will be like Jesus Christ who prayed: Father forgive them for they know not what they do. And we will be like our Father in heaven who pour down rain on the wicked and the just. When you decide to forgive and pray for those who offend you, you take back your power and reclaim your life.

God does not love us because of who we are but because of who He is. We should also love others unconditionally as God loves us. God loves us anyway. It does not matter who we are and what color we are. "For God so loved the world that He gave His only begotten Son, that whoever believeth in Him should not perish, but have everlasting life" (John 3:16). If God love us so much, we should love others genuinely. "The Lord hath appeared of old unto me, saying, Yea, I have loved thee with an everlasting love; therefore, with lovingkindness have I drawn thee" (Jeremiah 31:3). Honor God in your relationships. Paul in writing to the Colossians says, "But above all these things, put on love, which is the bond of perfection" (Colossians 3:14). Our Father, who gave His Son to die for us is waiting for us to bestow this kind of love to all around us even when they do not treat us well or have even abused, abandoned, betrayed deceived or manipulated us. We should make sure we have boundaries but show love to all around us so they can know we are children of our Almighty Father. Love trumps hate. Love is the best antidote for hatred. The Spirit that gives Jesus Christ the strength to endure the cross will enable us to draw on His strength to love and be of service to others. So, Speak the truth in love and grow in His knowledge everyday (Ephesians 4:15). May God give us the power to sacrifice our lives and carry our cross out of love for Jesus Christ and thereby love others through His bestowed loving power. Amen (Luke 9:23-24). Forgive those who have mistreated you so you can live fully physically and spiritually (Luke 23:34; Mark 11:25 Matthew 18:22). Forgiveness shuts the door on our past as Paul said in Philippians 3 verse 13. It is only when you let the past go that you will be able to embrace your future. And love your enemies (Luke 6:27). Let the God of the Universe who rights wrongs vindicate you and heal the wounds of your past. Do not fight for yourself because God says vengeance is mine, I will repay (Isaiah 35:4; Romans 12:

19; 1 Peter 3:9; Psalm 37:1). Trust God. He will right, all wrongs against you when you pray and show love even to those who despitefully treat you. And be sure that He will also protect you from their wicked plans. God will sustain you to the end. No evil will befall us if we love and forgive and put our trust in our Creator. The Word of God says, "when a man's ways please the Lord, He makes even his enemies to be at peace with him" (Proverbs 16:7). So, love and show kindness by being compassionate and caring for others (1 John 4:12 & 17). Let us love by being kind and compassionate, serving and caring for others (1 John 4:12 &17; John 3:16). But be careful not to become "amateur Providence" (Oswald Chambers) or the "Director of the Universe" (Everyday With Jesus), in other people's lives. In other words, let God be God in the lives of all the people you are interacting with, whether within or outside your family. Let God show you when to act and when to let God take control of other people's lives.

CHAPTER 9

Pursue your goals.

Remember, God gave you talents and make you in His image. God, who created us intricately made us for a unique purpose (2 Timothy 1:9; Psalm 139). God has given each of us a "one of a kind" personality, talent, gifting, abilities, purpose, calling and endowment. You are unique and "one of a kind" creation. The "I Am that I Am" uniquely created you to be a success in the world. You are the only person like you in the universe. There is no other person that has your fingerprints, your talents, your individuality or intelligence. So, don't miss the path God has mapped out personally for you here on earth. Your life's purpose has been ordained by the Almighty. Do not waste your God-given talents. What do I want to be when I grow up? Ask God? Pray and heed His direction and you will be on your way to successful life pursuit because you are the apple of God's eye. God sings over you and celebrates who you are because you are fearfully and wonderfully made in His image as I wrote earlier. God loves you just the way you are. God is a

God of second and more chances and He relishes in new beginnings. God created you to worship and communicate with Him. He even instructed us not to worship man-made gods (Exodus 20:4-5).

The greatest secret is for us to follow the will of God fully for our lives then our lives will become meaningful and we will find perfect freedom, because Jesus has come to give us life and this life more abundantly (John 10:10). Joseph, Moses and Daniel followed and stayed in God's will for their lives. God made good on His promises for them. He will do the same for you. Keep your focus on God He cannot fail you. Have a vision, write it down and pray incessantly for the vision to be manifested because "where there is no vision the people perish (Proverbs 29:18). Proverbs 16 verse 9 says a man's heart plans his (or her) way but the Lord directs (her or) his steps. "In the drama of life, God is the director behind the scenes" (Dave Branon, Our Daily Bread Ministries). Moses began his ministry at the age of eighty while Esther started hers as a teenage girl. God puts you into the school of faith to make sure you master what plans He has laid out for you. God is more interested in your character than in your comfort. Your character and integrity are the production of God's masterpiece. Daniel cared more about God's standards and laws than his own need for comfort or his life. As a result, God gave Daniel insight and understanding (Daniel 9:22). Mary, Jesus' mother was a simple young lady, whose only qualification was her willingness and trust in God Almighty. Mary's heart was right for God's fertile ground to become the young mother of Our Lord Jesus Christ.

Not following the will of God will only result in suffering, pain and spiritual and physical death. When we pursue the will of God, we have robust spiritual health, the joy of the Lord will be our strength (Nehemiah 8:10) and we can fulfill our destiny and utilize our talents fully (1 Corinthians 15:28). Work hard, be diligent and persevere as you pursue your God-given goals and work. Pursue Godly living and do not be wise in your own eyes. Beware of stubbornly pursuing your own goals without the assistance of the Holy Spirit so you do not end up in misery. Since our identity is hidden in Jesus Christ (Colossians 3:3), we should rely solely on His direction and follow His roadmap. God, the God of impossibility absolutely loves to make ordinary people become extraordinary.

The joy of the Lord will be our strength when we fulfill His purpose for our lives and do what He has ordained us to do. In other words, we do what He has created us to do and be what He has sent us to earth for. Yes, you have been created like Esther was (Esther 4:14) to fulfill God's purpose for this age. This means using our talents to glorify His Name here during our lifetime. Ecclesiastes 9 verse 10 says, "whatsoever your hand finds to do, do it with your might; for there is no work or device or knowledge or wisdom in the grave where you are going." In other words, do your best while you are alive to glorify God. Use all the opportunities that your Creator gives you while here on earth. So, be a man of valor like Gideon (Judges 6). Walk like a mighty warrior that God has made you in His absolute love and avoid delving on your insecurities and limitations. Remember, God has got the whole world in His Hands including you the reader of this book. And because He lives, you can face tomorrow. The simple truth is that you are not far away from His love, mercy and grace. He is therefore ready to bless you now and in the future. When God gives you a gift, He also gives you the grace and backs you with all capacities to use it and become a success.

Replace luck, coincidence and fate as words that you use with the 'powers of providence' in your daily vocabulary as a born-again child of God. What happens to you is not luck, co-incidence or fate but God's power and interventions that make things happen in your life. "The circumstances of a saint's life are ordained of God. In the life of a saint there is no such thing as chance. God by His providence brings you into circumstances that you can't understand at all, but the Spirit of God understands" (Oswald Chambers). God will always provide for and meet your needs as His child as you do your own part in the world. Paul says in Colossians 3 verse 23 that, "And whatever you do, do it heartily as to the Lord and not to men." Paul went on to say that you get your reward from God when you have a positive attitude to your work and use your talent to glorify Him and His Name and purpose on earth. So, let us aspire to dream God-ordained dreams and Our Father will make all grace abound towards us (2 Corinthians 9:8). God is after our hearts and we must relinquish our hearts to Him and keep nothing back from Him and He will redeem our souls. Give God His rightful place in your hearts and He will endow you with the rightful fulfilments on earth as your shepherd (Psalm 23) who cares for you, restores, renews your strength and guides you.

We should be careful not to be ambitious without God's will imbibe into our lives. Our ambition and zest for goals should be closely linked to God's will for our lives so we can have the joy of the Lord as we utilize our talents for His glory. And Paul supports this by saying that whatsoever you do, do it to the glory of God (1 Corinthians 10:31).

And when things do not work out as we have planned, we should still look to God and wait for His will to be manifested in our lives to move in another direction. After all He brought us here and will ensure we get to use our talents for His glory here. Look at Joseph, he used every God-given opportunity to glorify God by waiting solely for His plan to materialize. Even when he was jailed, he still patiently waited for God's will and purpose for his life. As the end of the story unfolds, God delivered him and esteemed him. "Life's challenges are not designed to break us but to bend us toward God" (Bill Crowder, Our Daily Bread Ministries). Oswald Chambers reiterated that, "we must continually maintain an adventurous attitude toward Jesus Christ, despite any potential risk." How comforting to be cognizant of the fact that we are held tightly in God's Hands, always cared for and loved and secure under His everlasting Arms (Isaiah 49:16; Psalm 17:8; Deuteronomy 31:6; 33:27). Establish some clearly objective goals for your life. This will give you some motivation to get up in the morning and give you satisfaction when you put your head on the pillow at night. So, go ahead, try something new. Prayerfully, aspire to do the impossible with God's infinite, provident and mighty guidance and direction. Set your goals in prayer and ask for

God's help and intervention (Philippians 3:14). God's grace is sufficient for us (2 Corinthians 12:9). Learn to wait on the Lord during difficulties, trials, sufferings and schooling as these are God's way of preparing you for the works He wants you to do for Him. God will equip you by refining your character in the process during the preparation. God says, "I will instruct you and teach you in the way you should go" (Psalm 32:8). You will have more faith and develop patience through perseverance (James 1:4). His presence and purpose are greater than our problems and pains. We can depend solely on God the infinite to be the same forever (Hebrews 13:8).

Therefore, live a life of faithfulness that is hidden in Jesus Christ, to be a success in the world. Bear fruit to glorify His Name with your talents (Psalm 1; Jeremiah 17:7-8). Because every good and perfect gift is from above (James 1:17). You have been created to make a difference in the world. As nobody else has your fingerprints in the world, nobody else has your talent. God has endowed you with unique gifts, talents and experiences. David had the sling and the stones in his hands. He used these to slay Goliath (1 Samuel 17:34-35; 45). Rely solely on God and what He gave you in your hands to slay the giants in your life. Moses had the rod and he used it perform miracles in front of Pharaoh and to part the Red Sea. Do not covet or wish for what is in someone else's hand because God has given you the right weapon you need to fight and win the battles of life and lead a fulfilled God-inspired life (Isaiah 35:4). Resist coveteousness and comparisons. Do not base your self-worth on material or worldly possessions, prestige, popularity, power, reputation or on certain relationships or company. Rely on your Creator. He brought you here to be a success. This is exactly what you should be and what you are going to be. And as Jabez went to the Creator of his life in his prayers (1 Chronicles 4:10), you also should go to your Creator, your source, with your prayers for direction for your life and He will reward you (Isaiah 43:1; Jeremiah 32:19). Know God closely and immerse yourself in His Word to obtain a solid identity. God loves and accepts you, that should make you shout Halleluia ! Be drawn closely to God so you can enjoy His blessings, favor, pleasure and His delight. "Delight yourself in the Lord and He will give you the desires of your heart" (Psalm 37:4),

Sure, there will be disappointments and obstacles. When these come, your reliance on God will get you through them that will make you develop the confidence you need to over-come them (Luke 1:30; 1 Peter 5:10; John 16:33). Therefore, be totally dependent on God and put all your confidence in your Creator. When all else fails trust in the Lord (Psalm 34:10; Ephesians 3:20; Philippians 3:8; 4:19; Isaiah 1:19 and Psalm 5:12). And even though you might not know what the future holds you should confidently believe in the One who holds the future. As Augustine informed us, "trust the past to the mercy of God, the present to God's love, and the future to God's provi-dence." God has got our past covered, our future secured and He's got more than enough grace for us for today.

As Christians, you also have the Word of God and prayer as your weapons that will aid you as you use the talent God has given you. So, go for it, use your unique God-endowed talent to glorify and showcase your Heavenly Father as Esther, Daniel and Joseph did. "Put your hope in the Lord now and always" (Psalm 131:3). Know who you are, do not think too highly of yourself. Think of yourself in proportion to who God created you to be, because God is your power, source, confidence and hope. Acknowledge God for who He is and give Him reverence. Lift Him up in your life and trust Him to give you His best in His time. Put your whole trust in the Lord and humbly pursue Him all the days of your life.

Let us aspire to please God in our daily walks and work (1 Thessalonians 2:4). Allow the Holy Spirit to make you more like Jesus Christ, who knows us best and loves us the most. Have faith and be a role model for both believers and unbelievers. God wants to use you and utilize your talents for His glory. Be an example to the next generation in words, deeds and actions. Lift them up like Paul did to Timothy.

But beware of dream killers and avoid being people pleasers but God pleaser. Dream killers are there to discourage you before you start to pursue the dreams God has given you. Pray that God deliver you from the fear of people (Isaiah 41:10). Rely on God to help you fulfill your dreams and use your God-given talents and gifts. God's purpose alone should be the stuff of which your dream is made. Since our lives are hidden in Jesus Christ, step out in faith, be focused on Him, be patient and commit your ways to the Lord and your Creator will make you succeed. Be bold. Follow God's plan and opportunities as they become available to you. Although there will be obstacles and tests, do not delve on regrets or self-pity. Do not listen to negatively inclined people, critics and those who complain but have no positive solutions in place. Pick friends who respect your values. This will prevent you from compromising to settle for less and therefore tarnish your integrity to satisfy your new friends. Settle for God's best, nothing less. Use your talents to glorify your Maker's goal for your life. Winston Churchill and those who put their trust solely in God never gave up. They pursued their God-given goals to the end of their lives. Winston Churchill even won a Nobel Prize in Literature after World War II. This means as a child of the Almighty you can always begin again and achieve His aim for your life even after Satan and its cohorts thinks you cannot make it. For God knows the thoughts He has for you and He will give you an expected and successful end (Jeremiah 29:11-13). If the ruler of the universe has excellent thoughts towards you, you are in excellent hands. If you do not abdicate your position as His child, you will reign here on earth and eternally with Him. You are an important part of His universe. God is always in the business of making so-called nobodies into somebodies; transforming wimps into warriors and cowards into giant killers. Jesus turns our despair into hope. God who created you for a purpose will work all things together in your life. As children of God expect great things from the Lord because God will not withhold good things from His children who walk uprightly (Psalm 84:11; Jeremiah 33:3). Your prayers should be that God give you the inspiration and God-endowed ambition to fulfill the purpose for which you were born and made in His own image. Shout for joy today because God Almighty is your Papa. You have been given talents as mandates to use to glorify God here on earth. Use your talents and be grateful for them. Beginning today, enjoy God. Enjoy the life that God has given you because the people who know their God shall be strong, and carry out great exploits (Daniel 11:32). God is our strength and shield. Approach each day with a sense of direction and purpose and cultivate a positive, creative, optimistic, courageous, adaptable and flexible state of mind to issues, challenges and problems that come your way. And dare to dream. Harriet Tubman said that: "every great dream begins with a dreamer."

CHAPTER 10

God says: Multiply and replenish the earth.

This applies to those that are married and those that are single like Paul. Be a Godly parent: spiritually and physically. We should encourage our children. And that means, those that we give birth to physically and spiritually. Paul encouraged Timothy and brought him up in the fear and admonition of the Lord (1 Timothy 1:2). So, do the same for your children. Do not grieve your children. Love them and discipline them, believe in them and cheer them on in the battle of life. Train them up in the fear and admonition of the Lord and when they are old they will not depart from God's way (Proverbs 22:6). So, "do not withhold correction from a child. For if you beat him with a rod, he will not die" (Proverbs 23:13). Correct your child. Speak wisdom into their ears and hearts. Teach and imbibe into them the Word of God (Deuteronomy 6:5-9) and assist them to put their life experiences into proper perspectives when they leave their comfort zones and take risks. You can do this by listening to them and giving them Godly advice and offer them options to grow. There are times when children wander like the prodigal. Be assured that the Word of God and the Spirit of God will redirect them to refocus. Let there be boundaries and teach them the fear and admonition of the Lord. Help them as they inculcate Godly values and principles. Take time to nurture, care and provide for both their physical, emotional, mental and spiritual needs.

Love them genuinely as God loves you. Do not abuse them or use languages that are ungodly. As Moses told the Israelites, pass the Godly touch to them as the next generation. Then you can say like Joshua said: As for me and my house we will serve the Lord (Joshua 24:15c).

Lead your spiritual and physical children to the Lord at a tender age. Teach them the fear, admonition and ways of the Lord early and when they are old they will not depart from the Lord's way. Constantly check on your children's spiritual growth in the Lord from time to time.

Encourage, teach, direct, instruct and admonish. Be a good example in word and actions as you use the Word of the Bible as precepts in your teachings and daily interactions. Help them grow and flourish in the Lord all their lives and you would have left a lasting heritage as God instructed the Israelites to do for their children. Discourage and direct them not to be unequally yoked with unbelievers. Give them room to grow in the Lord and in their lives. Instill words of wisdom into their lives by encouraging them to read the Word of God and through prov-erbs, wise sayings and from archives of experience. Encourage them to tap into their God-given resources and talents and abilities to help other citizens of the world. Instill confidence into their lives. Help them develop Godly character and integ-rity. Watch them grow in the fear and admonition of the Lord. Please note that educational achievements without instill-ing the fear of the Lord with Godly characteristics is useless. Imbibe in them that following the Lord is the best and only way to live a successful life forever. Lloyd George, a former British Prime Minister reiterated that "education without God makes clever devils." Only the inspiration of God's Word into a child's life can make them live life well and to the full.

Being a parent is like being a steward and taking care of someone that God gave us to care for. We are not the owners of those children God has commissioned us to care for. Because, before God made our children, He knew them and commis-sioned them for great things like He informed Jeremiah (Jeremiah 1:5-9; Psalm 139:13). They were created for a Godly purpose and have a destiny that has been designed solely by the Almighty. We should therefore look to God to help us do the job He has entrusted to us. It is an assignment. We should be prayerful as we nurture, guide and teach and direct the young ones through life. God always helps. He is able. Dedicate them to the Lord at a young age and release them to God when it is time for them to fly like the eaglet that is let out of the nest.

CHAPTER 11

Preach the Word in season and out of season with words and actions: while talking, while silent.

We are saved as Christians to tell others about God's grace in our lives. Jesus told us to go into the world and make disciples. As Christians we should preach the Word through our words and actions because the world needs redemption from sin and they are watching us. This is because, "they that be wise shall shine as the brightness of the firmament; and they that turn many to righteousness as the stars for ever and ever" (Daniel 12:3). "The fruit of the righteous is a tree of life. And he (or she) who wins soul is wise" (Proverbs 12:30) and she or he will win the victor's crown. Many people are going to hell because we are looking away or not paying attention to our commission to go into the world. The harvest is ripe all over the world. Take advantage of this from your backyard to the ends of the world. All of us are missionaries and God's representatives. We just do not take advantage of this fact. Your home, office, supermarket where you shop, the restaurant where you eat, your classroom, and your neighborhood are your pulpits. Take advantage of this when you check out or meet a waiter or teach or interact during office hours to tell others about Jesus Christ. You don't need to carry a Bible and you do not need to be an ordained minister. Your life is the Bible you need and that is what everyone around you will see. Your testimony is your sermon and your character and behavior are the avenues for evangelism (Mark 5:19) especially when it is backed by an honest, warm, Christ-centered lifestyle. So, go ahead and boldly tell others about the Man of Galilee and all He has done for you. This reminds me of a song I love to sing in Sunday School when I was young. "I love that man of Galilee, for He has done so very much for me. He has forgiven me all my sins and gave the Holy Ghost to me. I love that man of Galilee." So, tell people and everyone as I do that you love that man of Galilee. Speak words of love and encouragement to everyone God puts in your daily paths (Proverbs 16:24). Weep with those who weep (Romans 12:15) and comfort those who are in distress. And when you win souls your crown is waiting for you. So, share the Word, someone is listening. Someone is watching.

Influence your world, this is why you have been created and saved by the Precious Blood of Jesus Christ. Just follow God's direction when you tell others about your beloved Jesus Christ and give all the glory in your life to God Almighty who gave you the power and the ability to witness and to be here (Isaiah 42:8; Psalm 115:1). Remember the reason God has blessed you is so that you might bless others He brings into your life. Look for opportunities to show intentional kindness to others who are hurting and discouraged (Galatians 6:10), as God shows you kindness. Make a difference in somebody's life daily because you are wearing the fragrance of Jesus Christ (2 Corinthians 2:15). This fragrance comes from having a close relationship with Jesus Christ. Let everyone know that you have been with Jesus. That He is your Lord and Savior. Do not be discouraged if you do not see the result right away. Our Father will bring the increase at His own time as Paul said in 1 Corinthians 3 verse 6. Keep in mind the Word in Colossians 3 verse 12 that says that you should clothe yourself with compassion, kindness, humility, gentleness, and patience. Let compassion help you relate to different types of people. Testimony of the woman at the well in John 4 verse 39 who informed others about a man "who knew everything she ever did" was a gateway to the disciples' evangelism with the Samaritans. Be strong, be bold and be of good courage as you tell others about Our Savior Jesus Christ. We should work to combat the work of the thief (the devil), who only comes to kill, steal and destroy and be like Jesus Christ who came to give life more abundantly (John 10:10). Tell the world that Jesus is out to save and that Satan is out to destroy everything God has endowed them with. Let your words reflect Christ's message and let the way you live show the world His character. Evangelize with everything God has given you as your spiritual weapon: Praise, Prayer, the Word of God and fellowship with other believers.

Jesus modelled for us to welcome sinners through His parable of the prodigal son (Luke 15:13). God does not want us to be judgemental like the Pharisees and the older brother portrayed in the story. We should be welcoming and non-judgemental as we approach and invite those who are unlike us to Jesus Christ. May Jesus help us to see all the relationships and circumstances of our lives as possible times to evangelize Amen. Ensure that you spend time with the Lord as you brighten other people's lives with the gospel of Jesus Christ so your labor is not in vain. Pay attention to all the details in your life so you are not moving on without a close relationship with Our Lord. May God keep us faithful and alert to know how to love him, have a close relationship with Him and with all those that matter in our lives and at the same time also work for Him. Amen. May God help us grow to be His mature son and daughter. Amen. Dear Lord, let everyone we interact with know that you are our strength and security and that God's grace is sufficient for us (2 Corinthians 12:8-10). Amen. "And whatever you do, do it heartily as to the Lord and not to men, knowing that from the Lord you will receive the reward of the inheritance; for you serve the Lord (Jesus) Christ" (Colossians 3:23-24). So, my brothers and sisters, I pray that God use you in His vineyard to save souls. Amen. Oswald Chambers informed us to "remember that (we) can never give another person what (we) have found, but (we) can cause him (or her) to have a desire for it." So, just live as a follower of Jesus Christ in front of others and they will thirst for what you have and become Jesus' followers too. Go ahead, strengthen, encourage, support, advice, and be a companion to others. Answer God's call to love, enrich, and light up the darkness in the world and tell others about God's miracles, love, faithfulness and goodness.

CHAPTER 12

Give generously to God inspired purposes and to others in need because you reap what you sow.

Use whatever God gives you to glorify His Name. This is because, "He who gives to the poor will not lack. But he who hides his eyes will have many curses" (Proverbs 28:27). "The generous soul will be made rich, and he who waters will also be watered himself" (Proverbs 11:25). Because with the measure you give you will also get back. "Honor the Lord with your possessions and with the first fruits of all your increase. So, your barns will be filled with plenty and your vats will overflow with new wine" (Proverbs 3:9-10). This does not end up in money alone. Use all your God-given talents to glorify His Name to others. Utilize whatever resources, time and talent to help others and thereby be the answer to their prayers (Proverbs 3:27; Hebrews 6:10). Unbelievers have been won to Jesus Christ through believers' gifts of their time, energy, money and talent. Have a generous spirit (Proverbs 11:25; Matthew 11:28; Acts 2:46b). In order to help people, you must love them, know what you have to offer, recognize their needs, and connect to them at the point of their need. God does not hate money but he does not like the misuse and love of money (1 Timothy 6:10). Paul referred to the love of money as the root of all kinds of evil in 1 Timothy 6 verse 10. Use God's-given money and resources to glorify His Name and advance His gospel on earth. The devil will not like you because of this fact. But God will protect you from him and its cohorts and also bless you. Pray and believe God to help you to become a blessing to those around you and to those who genuinely profess the name of the Lord. You are blessed for a reason so use your blessings for God inspired purposes.

Malachi instructed us in chapter 3 verses 5 to 12 that we should give generously to God's purpose and we shall be blessed. And we are also instructed to tithe of all the blessings God gives us (Deuteronomy 14:22). Do not withhold any of your blessings from God. Give and it shall be given back by God good measure shaken together and running over men and women will give back to you (Luke 6:38). Paul admonishes us to be willing to share our blessings and riches (1 Timothy 6:18).

Share your blessings here on earth because you shall reap what you sow (Galatians 6:7).

CHAPTER 13

Respect your bodies as God's temple.

Our bodies are God's gift to us. What we do with our bodies is our gift back to Our Creator. So, honor God by respecting your bodies (1 Corinthians 6:18-20). God said in His Word in 2 Corinthians 6 verses 16 to 18 that, you are the temple of the living God and that you were bought with the precious blood of Jesus Christ. And God has said, I will dwell in them (1 Corinthians 3:16). And walk among them. I will be their God, and they shall be my people. Therefore, come out from among them and be separate, says the Lord (2 Corinthians 6:17). Do not touch what is unclean. And I will receive you. I will be a Father to you. And you shall be My sons and daughters, Says the Lord Almighty" (2 Corinthians 6:17). Be careful about what you wear, eat, drink and do with your bodies. As Jesus Christ cast out the money changers from the temple of God so you should cast out uncleanliness and all unnecessary things and accessories from your body which is God's Temple. Cast out overeating, fornication, evil thoughts, lazy habits, coveteousness and the like, which are works of the flesh (Galatians 5:19-21; Ephesians 5:3) from your body and invite the fruits of the spirit into your life (Galatians 5:22-23). Some of the health and physical issues we have in life can be averted if we take care of what we eat and respect God's temple.

We are made in God's image and therefore bear some of God's qualities. We are endowed with Supernatural, Calvary and Resurrection Powers because Jesus Christ who rose from the dead lives in us. So, respect the powers that have been bestowed into your lives by living a holy life. Consciously take care of your bodies as God's prices and possessions because our identity is hidden in Jesus Christ our Savior. Let the beauty of the Lord radiate in your lives as a born-again Christian for we are being transformed into His likeness with ever increasing glory (2 Corinthians 3:18).

Discipline your body (1 Timothy 4:8; 1 Corinthians 6:20; 9:27; Philippians 1:20) because your body is the temple of the Almighty God (1 Corinthians 6:19). Eat the right foods that are going to be of benefit to your body. Exercise and keep in shape so that all the organs of your body are healthy. Practice cleanliness every day. Dress modestly in a way that shows that you are a child of the Almighty. Take excellent care of the body that your Creator has given you. Also keep your heart pure and your face will radiate the glory of your Creator as you minister and interact with people. If your heart is pure, your body will be chaste. So, keep your heart pure with all diligence for out of it flows the issues of life (Proverbs 4:23). If your heart is pure your life will be pure. But if your heart and your thoughts are defiled, your life will be defiled.

Let the glory and beauty of God radiate from your heart and show through the glow of God in your face through the clothes and ardonments you wear as children of the Almighty.

CHAPTER 14

Have a heart of gratitude.

Gratitude is the soil on which spiritual joy thrives. Joanie Yoder of Our Daily Bread Ministries reiterated that, "an attitude of gratitude can make your life a beautitude." Be grateful to God and to all those who makes life meaningful for you. Be grateful at all times even when things and conditions look bleak and when there seems to be no hope and no light at the end of the tunnel. Thank God that you are still alive and enjoying His freely given air and all the good things He supplies. "Oh, that men would give thanks to the Lord for His goodness. And for His wonderful works to the children of men! For He satisfies the longing soul. And fills the hungry soul with goodness" (Psalm 107:8-9). Let men praise the name of the Lord for His Name is to be exalted and His glory is above the earth and heaven (Psalm 148:13). "Let everything that has breath praise the Lord. Praise the Lord" (Psalm 150:6). Look around for all He provides and seek His kingdom and wait for all other things to be added to you and your household (Matthew 6:33).

Wonderful and miraculous things happen when we show gratitude to God and when we find time to praise Our All-knowing Almighty Father (1 Chronicles 16:29 & 34). Jehoshaphat and the people of Judah utilized gratitude and praise to defeat their enemies through the help of God their Helper (2 Chronicles 20:21-22). Daniel gratefully acknowledged God in the midst of obstacle and unpredictability when his adversaries reported him to King Darius and God honored and rescued him from the lions' den as a result of his faith and gratitude (Daniel 6:10b & 1-29). Praise allows you to get God's favor and blessings. Paul and Silas, they prayed, they praised and the Holy Ghost came down. So, when the devil brings you face to face with trials and difficulties, just be grateful and praise His Holy Name and you will see His Hand move like He did for the people of Judah and for all those before and after that. I will praise you, Oh my Savior. I will praise you, Oh my Jesus. I will praise You, Oh my Savior. I will praise you forevermore. Halleluia ! It is when we praise God and show our gratitude to Him that He shows up with His blessings and protection. Be thankful for everything and don't take God and His daily blessings for granted. Recognize and receive God's blessings with grateful hearts (Psalm 103:1-2). His power will flow into your life when you show how grateful you are for His love and faithfulness. He created you and fearfully and wonderfully weave you together in your mother's womb (Psalm 139:14). This is something to shout and praise Him about. You are here on this earth. This is a reason to be grateful. We should give "thanks always for all things to God the Father in the name of Our Lord Jesus Christ submitting to one another in the fear of God" (Ephesians 5:20-21). Paul also encourages us in 1 Thessalonians 5 verse 18, to give thanks in everything because this is the will of God in Christ Jesus for us. We should give thanks to God all the time for His wonderful works to us as His children (Psalm 107:8). We should cultivate a heart of gratitude for what God has done in our lives so far, for what He is doing and for what He will still do. Say thanksgiving prayers every day. Paul in his writing to the Colossians 3 verse 17 says that, "And whatever you do in word or deed do all in the name of the Lord Jesus giving thanks to God the Father through Him." David C. McCasland of Our Daily Bread Ministries encouraged you that, "thankfulness depends on what is in your heart, not what is in your hand." Thanks be to God for giving us so much to be thankful for. Thank you, Lord for this opportunity to be here and for this one life you have given us.

Gratefulness depends solely our willingness to accept God's will for our lives. We need to accept that our Father, Almighty God can be trusted because He created us and therefore, He is in control of all that happens in our lives. His presence goes with us all day long. God is faithful and He is excellent. We can put our hope in Him to lift us through the strongest storm. Be dependent on God and His faithfulness and love. Always offer love and give thanks for His blessings and the storms that comes to us in life because our sufferings, challenges and obstacles draw us near to God. And they give us courage and strength to move on in life (Psalm 46:1). So, give thanks to Him because He will never fail you throughout your life's journey. Be grateful for His mercy and grace to sustain you and He will see you through because His love and mercy endure forever (Psalm 107:1 & 118:1) and He is good. Like I tell my friends: God is excellent all the time. He gives the best to His children and you are one of His precious children. The All-Powerful Lord of Heaven and Earth loves you. This is another reason to shout: Halleluia ! "Shout joyfully to the Lord, all the earth. Break forth in song, rejoice, and sing praise" (Psalm 98:4). The writer of Psalm 98 praised God for His salvation, His righteousness, His mercy and His faithfulness (verses 2-3). We have a lot to be thankful for. God is a faithful Father who takes excellent care of us His children. Always be grateful. A heart of gratitude leads to healthy life and spiritual vibrancy, growth and health. Anne Cetas of Our Daily Bread Ministries indicated that, "Gratitude should not be an occasional incident but a continuous (second by second) attitude." Acknowledge God's grace and goodness every second of your days here on earth. Downplay your self-interest when you give. Give God an acceptable offering from the bottom of your heart. Thanksgiving is a virtue that buds through practice.

In a quest to show God your gratitude, list all the basic things of life, the supports you receive from Him and others and the fact that you are alive and breathing and the ability to receive His blessings in your journal daily. Be grateful even for the opportunity to read His Word and this book. Let us bless the Lord at all times and let His praise continually be in our mouths (Psalm 34:1). We serve a living, faithful and joyous Lord. Let the world know through your joyful exuberance that we serve a living God and that you belong to Jesus. Daniel prayed prayers of gratitude in the midst of despair, fear and unpredictable situation (Daniel 6:10b) and God hears. Abel was grateful for God's provision and God smiled at his offering. Let us cultivate a heart of gratitude for what God has done in our lives, for what He is still doing and for all He promises to do in our lives in the future. Have a daily habit and attitude of gratitude prayers. Yes, You God are worthy of all praise, blessing, honor and glory in Jesus' Name Amen (Jeremiah 31:3-4; Genesis 29:30). Let us not forget that God provides us with all excellent things. As the years add up God's faithfulness and love multiplies. Praise God for all victories, seen and unseen. Whatever our age, let us make it a habit of thanking God for His greatness, help, provision and companionship. We should continue to praise God because He is in control of everything in our lives and we have nothing to fear. Worship God because of who He is and what He deserves (Psalm 29:2).

CHAPTER 15

Embrace the Word of God

Finally, the last but not the least, let us discuss embracing the Word of God. Thy Word Have I hidden in my heart that I might not sin against you (Psalm 119:11). Cherish the Word. Read it and ruminate on it while standing or sitting or walking. Memorize it. Use it against Satan and its cohorts as Our Savior did (Luke 4:1-13; Matthew 17:18-20) before He embarked on His mission as the emissary of God on earth. Chew on it as honey in your mouth (Psalm 119:103). Love it. Share it with fellow believers and with those who need to know Our Lord as their Savior and Lord and cherish His Ways. Psalm 119 is an excellent place to start. Proverbs and Ecclesiastes have words of wisdom embedded in them. The Psalms will lift up your spirits. The New Testament will inspire you. Stories of David, Joseph, Elijah, Elisha, Esther, Ruth, Abraham, Isaac, Jacob, Enoch, Noah, Caleb, Nehemiah, Peter, Paul, John, Mary the mother of Jesus, Lydia, Daniel, Shadrach, Meshach and Abednego to mention but a few of the characters in the Scripture, will keep you on your toes and encourage you. The life story of Job will stir up your faith to stand firm in the face of adversity and sufferings. Paul through the Epistles will not let you slumber. He will give you the Christian insights and inspirations to live your life in holiness by giving you practical suggestions and advice. The story of the Israelites in the Old Testament will encourage you and warn you against murmuring and idolatry. The Word will be a lamp to your feet (Psalm 119:105) and admonish you, instruct you, correct you (2 Timothy 3:16-17; Colossians 3:15). The Word encourages, nourishes and directs your paths as it did for Joshua (Joshua 1:5 & 8). Search it. Obey it. Find power and purpose in the Word.

As I have pointed out in all the chapters, find time to quietly study the Word every day. Set up a special time to read, think through the words you read and pray about what the Scripture imbibes into you. Then you and your household will be blessed as Psalm 1 verses 1 to 3; Joshua 1; Psalm 84 verse 12 and Jeremiah 17 verses 7 and 8 point out.

An important characteristic of a Christian is that she or he receives God's Word and act on it. Jesus said "for I have given to them (that is, His Disciples) the words which You have given Me; and they have received them, and have known surely that I came from You and they have believed that You sent me" (John 17:8). This applies to us as God's children and Jesus's new disciples here on earth. When we believe and receive the Word of God we will be blessed. Peter, one of the disciples, said in John

6 verse 68 that Jesus have the words of eternal life. One thing we should know is that "to obey the Word does not mean we will never have times of doubt and struggle, but that we hold on to it nevertheless" (Every Day with Jesus) and be directed and assisted by its truth. We should keep the Word, obey it as Jesus keeps us (1 John 2:3 & 1-17) and it will be well with us. Dave Branon of Our Daily Bread Ministries reiterated that God who is the arranger of our world and our society, revealed His desires for us through the Bible. The Scripture, compiled through the inspiration of the Holy Spirit, portrays information about how to live as God's children by obeying His rules and His standards. Proverbs 1 verse 7 says that the fear (and understanding the Word) is the beginning of knowledge (and wisdom, Godly character, living, prosperity and success). While Proverbs 30 verse 5 portrays that every Word of God is flawless and that God is a shield to those who take refuge in Him. We can take refuge by daily immersing ourselves in His Word. Good luck as you start eating the Word today as the bread of life, because God's Word is true and His heart is pure and kind (Psalm 33:4; Acts 14:17).

Conclusion

Alife spent in honoring the Lord throughout is a life well spent. So, pray, meditate, love, serve with all your heart. Pursue God and surrender to Him. Total surrender encouraged David to confront Goliath with nothing but a sling and five smooth stones. It inspired Joshua to lead the Israelites to the promised land. It gave Shadrach, Meshach and Abednego the faith to decline worshipping the king's God. This surrender embolden Moses to stand in front of Pharaoh in a household where he was raised as a son of Pharaoh's daughter to request that his brethren be "let go." It gave Noah the courage to build an Ark with naysayers putting him down left and right. It encouraged Paul to keep going amidst his enemies. It gave Daniel courage to stand and pray as his enemies look on in consternation and plot his death. It gave Joseph the courage to keep going when all odds were against him amidst trials and sufferings until God esteemed him to become the Prime Minister. There is Elijah, Elisha, Peter, Abraham, Jacob and so many others portrayed in God's Word. So, don't settle for lesser things. Want God ! Pursue God ! Give God the key to your heart today. And you will be happy you did. Please God ! Become a friend of God like David ! Follow God ! Believe God ! Receive God ! Live like Jesus Christ ! Let God be the center of your living and life. Don't go back to the world like the rich ruler in Luke 18. Enjoy life abundantly here and live eternally with Our Lord. Let your life start telling others about the faithfulness and goodness of our Almighty Father. Be assured that He who can keep you on your feet standing tall (Jude 24), will stay closely by your side throughout your journey here on earth. And know this important thing: God is consistently loving and faithful. Once you put your faith and trust in Him you will never be the same again. So, go ahead try Him and your life will be changed like that of Abraham, Moses, Daniel, Elijah, Elisha, David, Paul and others including my humble self.

Have you ever thought about where you are going when you leave this temporary abode? Yes, believe me, you are going some-where and you will give account when you get there. So why don't you start living now in such a way as to get a welcome party from your Almighty Father, Jesus Christ, the Holy Spirit and all the hosts of heaven when you arrive in Heaven.

This book has given you some hints about how you can live spiritually whole as a child of Almighty God. The bottom line is that you now need first to accept Jesus as your Lord and Savior, if you have not yet done so. Bow your head now wherever you are and pray that Jesus come into your heart. It is this simple. Believe me you will never be the same again after this prayer.

Tell a born again Christian that Jesus is now your Savior, get yourself a Holy Bible and find a Bible preaching church to buttress your faith and commitment. Welcome to a new journey to your heavenly home where your Papa is waiting for you after you finish your race here on earth. Be blessed today and every day. And May the joy of the Lord be your strength. Amen.

www.ingramcontent.com/pod-product-compliance
Lightning Source LLC
Chambersburg PA
CBHW032013040426
42448CB00006B/620